W9-BUU-714

The Book of
Comfort

THE BOOK OF

Comfort

The Perfect Daily Companion

H.K. Suh

BLACK DOG
& LEVENTHAL
PUBLISHERS
NEW YORK

Copyright © 2003 Black Dog and Leventhal Publishers

All rights reserved. No part of this book may be reproduced in any form or by any electronic or
mechanical means including information storage and retrieval systems without the written
permission of the copyright holder.

Published by
Black Dog & Leventhal Publishers, Inc.
151 West 19th Street
New York, NY 10011

Distributed by
Workman Publishing Company
708 Broadway
New York, NY 10003

Manufactured in Hong Kong

Cover and interior design by Sheila Hart Design
Cover photograph courtesy Corbis

ISBN 1-57912-335-x

h g f e d c b a

Library of Congress Cataloging-in-Publication Data available on file.

Contents

EVERYDAY COMFORTS
7

HOPE, LOVE, AND DREAMS
91

OVERCOMING ADVERSITY
159

PERSISTENCE
219

Everyday Comforts

Gently remind yourself that life
is okay the way it is, right now.
In the absence of your judgment,
everything would be fine.
As you begin to eliminate your
need for perfection in all areas
of your life, you'll begin to discover
the perfection in life itself.

Richard Carlson,

Don't Sweat the Small Stuff

There is no duty we so much underrate as
the duty of being happy. By being happy we
sow anonymous benefits upon the world.

Robert Louis Stevenson

Your diamonds are not
in far distant mountains or
in yonder seas;
they are in your own backyard,
if you but dig for them.

Russell H. Conwell

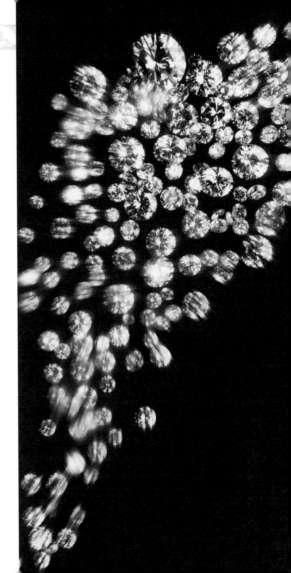

You have a solemn obligation to take care of yourself
because you never know when the world will need you.

Rabbi Hillel

The greatest discovery of my generation
is that a human being can alter his life
by altering his attitude.

William James

Just play. Have fun. Enjoy the game.

Michael Jordan

Just trust yourself,

then you will know how to live.

Johann Wolfgang von Goethe

Seek not outside yourself, heaven is within. Mary Lou Cook

My after forty face felt far more comfortable
than anything I lived with previously.
Self-confidence was a powerful beauty-potion;
I looked better because I felt better.
Failure and grief as well as success and love
had served me well. Finally, I was tapping into
that most hard-won of youth dews: wisdom.

Nancy
Collins

Your thorns are the best part of you.
Marianne Moore

Since we cannot change reality,

let us change the eyes which see reality.

Nikos
Kazantzakis

Leave something good
in every day.

Dolly Parton

Because our gifts carry us out into the
world and make us participants in life,
the uncovering of them is one of the most
important tasks confronting any one of us.

Elizabeth O'Connor,

Eighth Day of Creation:
Gifts and Creativity

No one can make you feel inferior without your consent.

Eleanor Roosevelt

Infinite riches are all around you if you will open your mental eyes and behold the treasure house of infinity within you. There is a gold mine within you from which you can extract everything you need to live life gloriously, joyously, and abundantly.

Joseph Murphy

We have all probably noted those sudden moments of quiet—those strange and almost miraculous moments in the life of a big city when there is a cessation of traffic noises—just an instant when there is only the sound of footsteps which serves to emphasize a sudden peace. During those seconds it is possible to notice the sunlight, to notice our fellow humans, to take breath.

Dorothy Day, pacifist

People from a planet without flowers would think we must be mad with joy the whole time to have such things about us.
Iris Murdoch

Searching is half the fun: life is much more manageable when thought of as a scavenger hunt as opposed to a surprise party.
Jimmy Buffett

I feel that a genuine, affectionate smile
is very important in our day-to-day lives.
How one creates that smile largely
depends on one's own attitude.
It is illogical to expect smiles from others
if one does not smile oneself. Therefore,
one can see that many things depend
on one's own behaviour.

His Holiness the Dalai Lama

★

People tell me I look good these days. I look good
because I feel good. I know people who are older
than I am who are twenty-five…. It's all about attitude.
To me, age is just a number.

Rita Moreno

I often get that question, "Up there, do you feel closer to God?" I think you feel closer to God holding the hand of someone in great pain who needs you. I feel closer watching a baby cry. There are thousands of ways. Traveling two hundred miles anywhere doesn't put you farther or closer to anything. What I cherish is all the ways it stretched and taught and grew and educated and shaped and refined me.

Kathryn Sullivan,
first American woman to walk in space

If you can react the same way to winning
and losing, that's a big accomplishment…

Chris Evert Lloyd

Happiness is a perfume you cannot pour on others without
getting a few drops on yourself.

Ralph Waldo Emerson

Do not look back in anger, or forward
in fear, but around in awareness.

James Thurber

The high note is not the only thing.
Placido Domingo

We are not human beings on a spiritual journey.
We are spiritual beings on a human journey.

Stephen Covey

When you acknowledge the less than perfect parts of yourself, something magical begins to happen. Along with the negative, you'll also begin to notice the positive, the wonderful aspects of yourself that you may not have given yourself credit for, or perhaps even been aware of.

Richard Carlson, *Don't Sweat the Small Stuff*

From what we get, we can make a living;
what we give, however, makes a life.

Arthur Ashe

❖

When I learn something new — and it
happens every day — I feel a little more
at home in this universe, a little more
comfortable in the nest.

Bill Moyers

Life is a great big canvas,
and you should throw all
the paint on it you can.

Danny Kaye

Oh, the places you'll go!

Dr. Seuss

❧

I read and walked for miles at night along the beach, writing bad blank verse and searching endlessly for someone wonderful who would step out of the darkness and change my life. It never crossed my mind that that person could be me.

Anna Quindlen

❧

The moment of victory is much too short
to live for that and nothing else.

Martina Navratilova

Achievement is the knowledge that you
have studied and worked hard and done
the best that is in you. Success is being
praised by others. That is nice but not as
important or satisfying. Always aim for
achievement and forget about success.

Helen Hayes

✳

In the arena of life the honors and rewards fall to those
who show their good qualities in action.

Aristotle

The one lesson I have learned is that
there is no substitute for paying attention.

Diane Sawyer

✳

I make the most of all that comes,
And the least of all that goes.

Sara Teasdale

No man is an island, entire of itself; every man is a piece of the continent.

John Donne

I skate to where the puck is going to be,
not to where it has been.

Wayne Gretzky

✳

We all have big changes in our lives that are
more or less a second chance.   Harrison Ford

The happiness of life is made up of minute fractions—the little, soon-forgotten charities of a kiss or smile, a kind look, a heart-felt compliment, and the countless infinitesimals of pleasurable and genial feeling.

Samuel Taylor Coleridge

Make one person
happy each day and in
forty years you will have
made 14,600 human
beings happy for a
little time, at least.

Charley Willey

Happy [is] the man who has learned the
cause of things and has put under his feet
all fear, inexorable fate, and the noisy
strife of the hell of greed.

Virgil

Happiness is not a station to arrive at,

but a manner of traveling.

Margaret Lee Runbeck

Speak the truth.
Give whatever you can.
Never be angry.
These three steps will lead you
Into the presence of the gods.

Buddha

The art of living does not consist
in preserving and clinging to a particular
mode of happiness, but in allowing
happiness to change its form without
being disappointed by the change;
happiness, like a child, must be allowed
to grow up.

Charles L. Morgan

Normal day, let me be aware of the treasure you are. Let me learn from you, love you, bless you before you depart. Let me not pass you by in quest of some rare and perfect tomorrow. Let me hold you while I may, for it may not always be so. One day I shall dig my nails into the earth, or bury my face in the pillow, or stretch myself taut, or raise my hands to the sky and want, more than all the world, your return.

Mary Jean Iron

Yes, there is a Nirvana: it is in leading your sheep
to a green pasture, and in putting your child to sleep,
and in writing the last line of your poem.

Kahlil Gibran

❖

When I first open my eyes upon the morning
meadows and look out upon the beautiful
world, I thank God I am alive.

Ralph Waldo Emerson

❖

Let the thankful heart
sweep through the day and,
as the magnet finds the iron,
so it will find, in every hour,
some heavenly blessings!

Henry Ward Beecher

The best things are nearest: breath in your nostrils,
light in your eyes, flowers at your feet, duties at
your hand, the path of God just before you.
Then do not grasp at the stars, but do life's plain,
common work as it comes, certain that daily duties
and daily bread are the sweetest things of life.

Robert Louis Stevenson

★

Just to be is a blessing. Just to live is holy.

Abraham Heschel

Life is the first gift, love is the second, and understanding the third.

Marge Piercy

✦

A thankful heart is not only the greatest
virtue, but the parent of all other virtues.

Cicero

Friendship is the only cement that will
ever hold the world together.

Woodrow Wilson

Friends are an aid to the young, to guard them from error;
to the elderly, to attend to their wants and to supplement
their failing power of action; to those in the prime of life,
to assist them to noble deeds.

Aristotle

Cast thy bread upon the waters:
for thou shalt find it after many days.

Ecclesiastes 11:1

✹

O how sweet it is to enjoy life,
Living in honesty and strength!

And wisdom is sweet,
And freedom

Buddha

✹

The loftiest edifices need the deepest foundations.

George Santayana

Human felicity is produced
not so much by great pieces
of good fortune that
seldom happen
as by little advantages
that occur every day.
Benjamin
Franklin

He who binds to himself a joy
Does the winged life destroy;
But he who kisses the joy as it flies
Lives in eternity's sun rise.

William Blake

✳

Eden is that old-fashioned House
We dwell in every day
Without suspecting our abode
Until we drive away

Emily Dickinson

✳

The ornament of a house is the friends who frequent it.

Ralph Waldo Emerson

The ache for home lives in all of us, the safe place where
we can go as we are and not be questioned.

Maya Angelou

Love yourself and watch—
Today, tomorrow, always.

To straighten the crooked
You must first do a harder thing—
Straighten yourself.

Buddha

Every one must form himself
as a particular being, seeking, however,
to attain that general idea of which
mankind are constituents. Johann Wolfgang von Goethe

My holy of holies is
the human body, health,
intelligence, talent,
inspiration, love, and
absolute freedom.

Anton Chekhov

Zest is the secret of all beauty.
There is no beauty that is
attractive without zest.

Christian Dior

Kindness it is that brings forth kindness always.

Sophocles

I do not cut my life up into days
but my days into lives, each day,
each hour, an entire life.

Juan Ramon Jimenez

Living well and beautifully and
justly are all one thing.

Socrates

There is health in table talk and nursery play.

We must wear old shoes and have aunts and cousins.

Ralph Waldo Emerson

The beautiful souls
are they that are universal,
open, and ready
for all things.

Montaigne

There is pleasure
And there is bliss.
Forgo the first to possess the second.

Buddha

_ᑯ

We can lift ourselves out of ignorance,
we can find ourselves as creatures of
excellence and intelligence and skill.
We can be free! We can learn to fly!

Richard Bach,
Jonathan Livingston Seagull

We carry with us the wonders we seek without us.

Sir Thomas Browne

One does not "find oneself" by pursuing one's self,
but on the contrary by pursuing something else and
learning through some discipline or routine
(even the routine of making beds) who one is
and wants to be.

May Sarton

Oft times nothing profits more
Than self-esteem, grounded on just and right
Well-managed.

John Milton

✳

Drink deeply.
Live in serenity and joy.

Buddha

Teach us Delight in simple things,
And Mirth that has no bitter springs.

❖   Rudyard Kipling

Success means we go to sleep at night
knowing that our talents and abilities
were used in a way that served others.

Marianne Williamson

There is satiety in all things, in sleep, and lovemaking,

in the loveliness of singing and the innocent dance.

Homer,
The Iliad

Health, contentment, and trust

Are your greatest possessions,

And freedom your greatest joy.

Buddha

To every thing there is a season,
and a time to every purpose
under the heaven.

Ecclesiastes 3:1

✳

Look on this beautiful world,
and read the truth
In her fair page.

William Cullen Bryant

Think naught a trifle, though it small appear;
Small sands the mountain, moments make the year,
And trifles life.   Edward Young

Rightly viewed no meanest object is
insignificant; all objects are as windows,
through which the philosophic eye looks
into infinitude itself.

Thomas Carlyle

Wherever life takes us, there are always moments of wonder.

President Jimmy Carter

Lead the life that will make you kindly and friendly to everyone about you, and you will be surprised what a happy life you will live.

Charles M. Schwab

To have that sense of one's intrinsic worth which constitutes self-respect is potentially to have everything.

Joan Didion

Faith in oneself...
is the best and safest course.

Michelangelo

Write it on your heart that every day is the best day in the year.

Ralph Waldo Emerson

One appreciates that daily life is really
good when one wakes from a horrible
dream, or when one takes the first outing
after a sickness. Why not realize it now?

William Lyon Phelps

My advice to you is not to inquire why or whither,
but just to enjoy your ice cream while it's on your plate.

Thornton Wilder

People say that what we're all seeking in life is a meaning for life.
I don't think that's what we're really seeking. I think that what
we're seeking is an experience of being alive, so that out life
expereience on the purely physical plane will have resonances
within our innermost being and reality, so that we actually feel
the rapture of being alive.

Joseph Campbell

Each friend represents a world in us;
a world possibly not born until they
arrive, and it is only in meeting them
that a new world is born.

Anaïs Nin

There is no need for temples,

no need for complicated philosophies.

My brain and my heart

are my temples;

my philosophy is kindness.

His Holiness the Dalai Lama

Tis a gift to be simple,

'Tis a gift to be free,

'Tis s gift to come down

Where we ought to be

And when we find ourselves

In the place that's right

'Twill be in the valley

Of love and delight

Shaker hymn

Take the gentle path.

George Herbert

Ah! There's nothing like staying home for real comfort.

Jane Austen

Work is not always
required. There is such a
thing as sacred idleness, the
cultivation of which is now
fearfully neglected.

George
Macdonald

Sit.
Rest.
Work.

Alone with yourself,
Never weary.

On the edge of the forest
Live joyfully,
Without desire.   Buddha

Not everything that can be counted, counts.

And not everything that counts can be counted.

Albert Einstein

It is inevitable when one has a great need
of something, one finds it. What you need
you attract like a lover.

Gertrude Stein

I am not bound to win, but

I am bound to be true.

I am not bound to succeed, but

I am bound to live up to

what light I have.

Abraham Lincoln

If thou workest at that which is before thee …

expecting nothing, fearing nothing, but satisfied

with thy present activity according to Nature,

and with heroic truth in every word and sound

which thou utterest, thou wilt live happy.

Marcus Aurelius

When you get to the end of your rope, tie a knot and hang on.
Franklin Delano Roosevelt

Quieten your mind.

Reflect.

Watch.

Nothing binds you.

You are free.

You are strong.
Buddha

If you want an accounting of your worth,
count your friends.

Merry Browne

✳

It is the intention, not the deed,
wherein the merit or praise
of the doer consists.

Peter Abelard

I desire … to leave this one great fact clearly stated.
THERE IS NO WEALTH BUT LIFE.

John Ruskin

※

Up! Up! my friend, and quit your books;
Or surely you'll grow double;
Up! Up! my friend, and clear your looks;
Why all this toil and trouble?

William Wordsworth

Let us dare to read, think, speak and write.

John Adams

✮

To know how to grow old is the masterwork
of wisdom, and one of the most difficult
chapters in the great art of living.

✮ Henri Frederic Amiel

The most useful piece of learning for the uses
of life is to unlearn what is untrue.

Antisthenes

Be able to be alone. Lose not the advantage of
solitude, and society of thyself.

Sir Thomas Browne

One has only to sit in the woods or fields, or by the shore
of the river or lake, and nearly everything of interest will
come round to him, the birds, the animals, the insects.

John Burroughs

The greatest friend of truth is Time,
her greatest enemy is Prejudice,
and her constant companion is Humility.

Charles Caleb Colton

Our life is a faint tracing on the surface of mystery, like the idle,
curved tunnels of leaf miners on the face of a leaf. We must
somehow take a wider view, look at the whole landscape, really see it,
and describe what's going on here. There we can at least wail
the right question into the swaddling band of darkness, or,
if it comes to that, choir the proper praise.

Annie Dillard

Some have too much, yet still do crave;

I little have and seek no more.

They are but poor, though much they have,

And I am rich with little store:

They poor, I rich; they beg, I give;

They lack, I leave; they pine, I live.

My wealth is health and perfect ease;

My conscience clear my chief defense;

I never seek by bribes to please,

Nor by deceit to breed offence:

Thus do I live; thus will I die;

Would all did so well as I.

Sir Edward Dyer

All through my life I never did believe in human measurement. Numbers, time, inches, feet. All are just ploys for cutting nature down to size. I know the grand scheme of the world is beyond our brains to fathom, so I don't try, just let it in.

Louise Erdrich

Personality, too, is destiny. Erik Erikson

It is not the possessor of many things
whom you will rightly call happy.
The name of the happy man is claimed
more justly by him who has learnt the
art whereby to use what the gods give.
Horace

What's a man's first duty?
The answer is brief: to be himself.

Henrik Ibsen

Love the Truth. Let others have their truth,
and the truth will prevail.

Jan Hus

Of all our possessions wisdom alone is immortal.

Isocrates

The greatest wealth is to live content
with little, for there is never want where
the mind is satisfied.

Lucretius

The lack of wealth is easily repaired but
the poverty of the soul is irreplaceable.

Montaigne

Man is born to live and not to prepare to live.

Boris Pasternak

I affirm that the good is the beautiful.

Socrates

We know nothing of tomorrow; our business is to be good and happy today.

Sydney Smith

Fortunate, indeed, is the man who takes exactly the right measure of himself, and holds a just balance between what he can acquire and what he can use, be it great or be it small.

Peter Mere Latham

❖

O Lord, support us all the day
long, until the shadows lengthen
and the evening comes, and the
busy world is hushed, and the
fever of life is over, and our work
is done. Then in thy mercy grant
us a safe lodging, and a holy rest,
and peace at the last.

Cardinal Newman

To live content with small means; to
seek elegance rather than luxury, and
refinement rather than fashion; to be
worthy, not respectable, and wealthy,
not rich; to study hard, think quietly,
talk gently, act frankly; to listen to stars
and birds, to babes and sages, with open
heart; to bear all cheerfully, do all bravely,
await occasions, hurry never. In a word,
to let the spiritual, unbidden and
unconscious, grow up through the
common. This is to be my symphony.

William Henry Channing

✳

Love your life, poor as it is. You may perhaps have some pleasant, thrilling, glorious hours, even in a poorhouse. The setting sun is reflected from the windows of the almshouse as brightly as from the rich man's abode.

Henry David Thoreau

Is it so small a thing
To have enjoyed the sun,
To have lived light in the spring,
To have loved, to have thought, to have done;
To have advanced true friends, and beat down baffling foes?

Matthew Arnold

There are two days in the week about which and upon which
I never worry. Two carefree days, kept sacredly free from fear
and apprehension. One of these days is Yesterday....
And the other day I do not worry about is Tomorrow.

Robert Jones Burdette

I do not hunger for a well-stored mind,
I only wish to live my life, and find
My heart in unison with all mankind.

Edmund Gosse

Let your boat of life be
light, packed with only
what you need—
a homely home and
simple pleasures, one or
two friends, worth the
name, someone to love
and someone to love you,
a cat, a dog, and a pipe
or two, enough to eat
and enough to wear, and
a little more than enough
to drink; for thirst is a
dangerous thing.

Jerome K. Jerome

The great man is he who does not lose his child's heart.

Mencius

A gourd of wine and a sheaf of poems—
A bare subsistence, half a loaf, no more—
Supplies us two alone in the free desert:
What sultan would we envy on his throne.

Omar Khayyam

Joy is peace dancing and peace is joy at rest.

F.B. Meyer

The same heart beats in every human breast.   Matthew Arnold

Little deeds of kindness,
Little words of love,
Help to make earth happy
Like the heaven above.

Julia A. Fletcher Carney

Truth is
the daughter
of time.

Aulus
Gellius

God of wilderness, God of wildness, lead me to
the quiet places of my soul. In stillness, in openness,
may I find my strength.

Jan Richardson

God helps them that help themselves.

Benjamin Franklin

HOPE, LOVE, AND DREAMS

Despite everything, I believe that people
are really good at heart.

Anne Frank

❧

Anyone who chooses to live their life in
Loving can change the world.

John-Roger

What makes the desert beautiful is that
somewhere it hides a well.

Antoine de Saint-Exupéry

Sometimes it's a form of love just to talk
to somebody that you have nothing
in common with and still be fascinated
by their presence.

David Byrne

There are always flowers for those who want to see them. Henri Matisse

The remedy for all blunders,
the cure of blindness,
the cure of crime, is love.

Ralph Waldo Emerson

It is above all by the imagination that we achieve
perception and compassion and hope.

Ursula K. Le Guin

If you want OTHERS to be happy, practice compassion. If YOU want to be happy, practice compassion. His Holiness the Dalai Lama

✳

Love is all we have, the only way that each can help the other. Euripides

Love is, above all, the gift of oneself.

Jean Anouilh

✳

[We pray to you], O God,
For strength, determination, and willpower,
to do instead of just to pray,
To become instead of merely to wish

Harold S. Kushner

Nobody has ever measured, not even poets,
how much the heart can hold.

Zelda Fitzgerald

Our aspirations are our possibilities.

Samuel Johnson

✷

Only the heart knows
how to find
what is precious.   Fyodor Dostoevsky

✷

It is only with the heart that one can see rightly,
what is essential is invisible to the eye.

Antoine de Saint-Exupéry

Hope is the belief, more or less strong, that joy will come.

Sydney Smith

Love is an irresistible desire
to be irresistibly desired.

Robert Frost

Do you want me to tell you something
really subversive? Love is everything
it's cracked up to be. That's why people
are so cynical about it. It really is worth
fighting for, being brave for, risking
everything for. And the trouble is,
if you don't risk everything,
you risk even more.

Erica Jong

Hope is faith holding out its hand in the dark.

George Iles

Hope is the positive
mode of awaiting
the future.

Emil
Brunner

Love makes your soul crawl out from its hiding place.

Zora Neale Hurston

In this world
Hate never yet dispelled hate.
Only love dispels hate.
This is the law,
Ancient and inexhaustible.

Buddha

Hope is not the conviction that something will turn
out well but the certainty that something makes sense,
regardless of how it turns out.

Vaclav Havel

To love oneself is the beginning of a life-long romance.

Oscar Wilde

Where there is great love
there are always miracles.

Willa Cather

For I believe in harbors at the end.

Thomas Wolfe

Hope is a waking dream. Aristotle

People who pray for courage, for strength to bear the unbearable, for the grace to remember what they have left instead of what they have lost, very often find their prayers answered. They discover that they have more strength, more courage than they ever knew themselves to have.

Harold S. Kushner

The greatest good you can do for others is not just to share your riches but to reveal to them their own.

Benjamin Disraeli

The best proof of love is trust.

Joyce Brothers

✳

You will find, as you look back upon your life, that the moments when you really lived are the moments when you have done things in the spirit of love.

Henry Drummond

Hope is like a road in the country;
there never was a road, but when many people walk on it,
the road comes into existence.

Lin Yutang, Chinese author and activist

Old age isn't so bad when you consider the alternatives.

Maurice Chevalier

Love is an act of endless
forgiveness, a tender look
which becomes a habit.

Peter
Ustinov

Let us learn to appreciate there will be
times when the trees will be bare, and
look forward to the time when we may
pick the fruit.

Peter Seller

Just as despair can come to one only from other human beings,
hope, too, can be given to one only by other human beings.

Elie Wiesel

We must accept finite disappointment,
but never lose infinite hope.

Martin Luther King, Jr.

There are only two ways to live your life.
One is as though nothing is a miracle.
The other is as though everything is a mira

Albert Einstein

Knowledge of what you love somehow comes to you;
you don't have to read or analyze nor study.
If you love a thing enough, knowledge of it seeps into you,
with particulars more real than any chart can furnish.

Jessamyn
West

For where your treasure is, there will your heart be also.

Matthew 6:21

May the road rise to meet you.

May the wind always be at your back.

May the sun shine warm upon your face.

And rains fall soft upon your fields.

And until we meet again, may God hold

you in the hollow of your hand.

Irish blessing

❖

Where there is life, there is hope. Talmud

❖

Hope is patience
with the lamp lit.
Tertullian

And thou shalt be secure because there is hope.

Job 11:18

❖

I am sure there is Magic in everything.

Frances Hodgson Burnett

Everything that is done in the world is done by hope.

Martin Luther

✳

The more I wonder, the more I love.　Alice Walker

Hope and patience are two sovereign remedies for all, the surest reposals, the softest cushions to lean on in adversity.

Robert Burton

Optimism is the faith that leads to achievement. Nothing can be done without hope or confidence.

Helen Keller

Talk not of wasted affection, affection never was wasted;
If it enrich not the heart of another, its waters, returning
Back to their springs, like the rain, shall fill them full of refreshment;
That which the fountain sends forth returns again to the fountain.

Henry Wadsworth Longfellow

We live in a wonderful world that is full
of beauty, charm and adventure. There is
no end to the adventures that we can have
if only we seek them with our eyes open.

Jawaharlal Nehru

I'm not afraid of storms,
for I'm learning to sail my ship.

Louisa May Alcott

If you feel positive, you have a sense of hope.

If you have hope, you can have courage.

Kathrine Switzer, pioneering marathon runner

★

He who bears in his heart
a cathedral to be built
is already victorious.

Antoine de Saint-Exupéry

The supreme happiness of life
is the conviction that we are loved.

Victor Hugo

Look for a lovely thing and you will find it,
It is not far—
It never will be far.

Sara Teasdale

No one is born hating another person because of the color
of his skin, or his background, or his religion. People must
learn to hate, and if they can learn to hate, they can be
taught to love, for love comes more naturally to the human
heart than its opposite.

Nelson Mandela

In times of trouble avert not thy face from hope,
for the soft marrow abideth in the hard bone.

Hafiz

We should not let our fears hold us back
from pursuing our hopes.

John F. Kennedy

★

No pessimist ever discovered the secrets of the stars,
or sailed to an uncharted land, or opened a new heaven
to the human spirit.

Helen Keller

Someday, after mastering winds, waves, tides and gravity, we shall harness the energy of love; and for the second time in the history of the world, man will have discovered fire.

Pierre Teilhard de Chardin, paleontologist and philosopher

We cannot do great things on this earth.
We can only do little things with great love.

Mother Teresa

❖

The more love you give, the more you will receive.
As you put more emphasis on being a loving person,
which is something you can control—and less emphasis
on receiving love, which is something you can't control—
you'll find that you have plenty of love in your life.
Soon you'll discover one of the greatest secrets
in the world: Love is its own reward.

Richard Carlson, *Don't Sweat the Small Stuff*

Familiar acts are beautiful through love.

Percy Bysshe Shelley

❖

He that is of
a merry heart hath
a continual feast.

Proverbs

True hope is swift and flies with swallow's wings;

Kings it makes Gods, and meaner creatures kings.

William Shakespeare

If you think you can, you can. And if you think you can't, you're right.

Mary Kay Ash

✫

No act of kindness, however small, is ever wasted.

Aesop

✫

Let me light my lamp, says the tiny star;
And never debate whether
It will dispel the darkness.

Rabindranath Tagore

✫

For small creatures such as we the vastness is bearable only through love.

Carl Sagan

If you feel that your
present way of life is
unpleasant or has some
difficulties, then don't
look at these negative
things. See the positive
side, the potential, and
make an effort.

His Holiness
the Dalai Lama

✳

The joyfulness of a man
prolongeth his days.

Psalms

Dwell upon the brightest parts of every prospect…
and strive to be pleased with the present circumstances.

Abraham Lincoln

Think of the ills from
which you are exempt.

Joseph
Joubert

Why worry? Look at all the things we
have and be happy. I can be happy just
sitting on a mountain.

Araceli Segarra,
mountain climber who reached the peak of Everest

He who limps still walks.

Stanislaw
Lece

❧

Think of all the beauty
still left around you
and be happy.

Anne Frank

❧

A pessimist sees the difficulty in every opportunity,
an optimist sees the opportunity in every difficulty.

Winston Churchill

Scenery is fine—but human nature is finer. John Keats

Say "Yes" to the seedlings and a giant forest cleaves the sky.

Say "Yes" to the universe and the planets become your neighbors.

Say "Yes" to dreams of love and freedom.

It is the password to utopia.

Brooks Atkinson

The essence of optimisim is that it
takes no account of the present,
but it is a source of inspiration,
of vitality and hope where others
have resigned; it enables a man to hold
his head high, to claim the future
for himself and not to abandon it
to his enemy.

Dietrich Bonhoeffer

Imagination is more important than knowledge.
Knowledge is limited. Imagination encircles the world.

Albert Einstein

Strong hope is a much greater
stimulant of life than any single
realized joy could be.

Friedrich
Nietzsche

However mean your life is, meet it
and live it; do not shun it and call it
hard names. It is not so bad as you are.
It looks poorest when you are richest.
The fault-finder will find faults even
in Paradise. Love your life.

Henry David Thoreau

Hope is a light diet, but very stimulating.

Honoré de Balzac

And love says
I will, I will take care of you
To everything that is
Near
Hafiz

Every man, every woman carries in heart
and mind the image of the ideal place,
the right place, the one true home,
known or unknown, actual or visionary.

Edward Abbey

In every child who is born, under no matter what circumstances, and of
no matter what parents, the potentiality of the human race is born again.

James Agee

For every thing that lives is holy, life delights in life;
Because the soul of sweet delight can never be defil'd.

William Blake

Every day, in every way,
I am getting better and better.
Emile Coue

And thou wilt give thyself relief, if thou doest every act
of thy life as if it were the last, laying aside all carelessness
and passionate aversion from the commands of reason,
and all hypocrisy, and self-love, and discontent with all
the portion which has been given to thee.

Marcus Aurelius Antonius

Too late is tomorrow's life; live for today. Martial, 2nd-century Roman poet

I am still learning.
Michelangelo

Life involves passions, faiths, doubts
and courage.
Josiah Royce

Remember that the most beautiful things
in the world are the most useless:
peacocks and lilies for instance.

John Ruskin

Sound, sound the clarion, fill the fife!
To all the sensual world proclaim,
One crowded hour of glorious life
Is worth an age without a name.

Sir Walter Scott

Begin at once to live, and count each separate day as a separate life.

Seneca

※

Every child comes with the message that
God is not yet discouraged of man.

Rabindranath Tagore

※

It is only when we forget
all our learning that we
begin to know.

Henry David
Thoreau

All human beings are born free and equal,
in dignity and rights.

Universal Declaration of Human Rights

✻

We must cultivate our garden.

Voltaire

I celebrate myself, and sing myself.

Walt Whitman

When I look at the world gently,
when I look at others the way
I have sometimes sensed that
Something looks at me,
I become a friend.
And there is no higher calling.

Hugh Prather, *Notes to Myself*

Listen to your life. See it for the fathomless mystery it is. In the boredom and pain of it, no less than in the excitement and gladness: touch, taste, smell your way to the holy and hidden heart of it, because in the last analysis all moments are key moments and life itself is grace.

Frederick Buechner

Where is God? Wherever you let God in. Hasidic saying

People ought not to consider so much what they are to do as what they are;
let them but be good and their ways and deeds will shine brightly.

Meister Eckhart

❖

When a man has
made peace with himself,
he will be able
to make peace in
the whole world.

Martin Buber

You don't get to choose
how you will die.
Or when. You can only
decide how you are going
to live. Now.

Joan Baez

If I am not for myself, who will be for me?

And if I am only for myself, what am I?

And if not now—when?

Rabbi Hillel

Nobody is perfect.

Look for the good in

others. Forget the rest.

Barbara Bush

The really important things in life can't be said, only shown.

Ludwig Wittgenstein

❦

Where'er you walk, cool gales shall fan the glade,
Trees, where you sit, shall crowd into a shade:
Where'er you tread, the blushing flow'rs shall rise,
And all things flourish where you turn your eyes.

Alexander Pope

For Mercy has a human heart,
Pity a human face,
And Love, the human form divine,
And Peace, the human dress.

William Blake

✴

As soon as you trust yourself, you will know how to live.

Johann Wolfgang von Goethe

✴

I expect to pass through this world but once; any good thing therefore that I can do, or any kindness that I can show to any fellow creature, let me do it now; let me not defer or neglect it, for I shall not pass this way again.

Etienne de Grellet

✳

The windows of my soul I throw
Wide open to the sun.

John Greenleaf Whittier

Be noble! and the nobleness that lies
In other men, sleeping, but never dead,
Will rise in majesty to meet thine own.

James Russell Lowell

Love is ever
the beginning of
Knowledge
as fire is of light.

Thomas Carlyle

Beauty will save the world. Fyodor Dostoevsky

All human wisdom is summed up
in two words: wait and hope.

Alexandre
Dumas

The most beautiful thing we can
experience is the mysterious.
It is the source of all art and science.

Albert Einstein

To know, to think, to dream. That is everything.

Victor Hugo

But when two people are at one in their innermost hearts,

They shatter even the strength of iron or of bronze.

And when two people understand each other in their inmost hearts,

Their words are sweet and strong, like the fragrance of orchids.

I Ching

Between Hope and Fear,
Love makes her home.

Ramon
Lully

Love is nothing but joy accompanied
with the idea of an eternal cause.

Baruch Spinoza

There is a land of the living

and a land of the dead

and the only bridge is love,

the only survival, the only meaning.

Thornton Wilder

An ounce of love is worth a pound of knowledge.

John Wesley

People throughout the world may look
different or have a different religion,
education, or position, but they are all
the same. They are the people to be loved.
They are all hungry for love.   Mother Teresa

Love conquers all things;
let us too surrender to Love.

Virgil

Love makes those young whom age doth chill,
And whom he finds young, keeps young still.

William Cartwright

Change everything, except your loves. Voltaire

Tis always morning somewhere in the world.

Richard Henry Horne

If you remember'd not the slightest folly
That ever love did make thee run into,
Thou hast not lov'd.

William Shakespeare

Let us have faith that right makes might, and in that faith
let us to the end dare to do our duty as we understand it.

Abraham Lincoln

OVERCOMING ADVERSITY

God does not cause our misfortunes. Some are caused by bad luck, some are caused by bad people, and some are simply an inevitable consequence of our being human and being mortal, living in a world of inflexible natural laws. The painful things that happen to us are not punishments for our misbehavior, nor are they in any way part of some grand design on God's part. Because the tragedy is not God's will, we need not feel hurt or betrayed by God when tragedy strikes. We can turn to Him for help in overcoming it, precisely because we can tell ourselves that God is as outraged by it as we are.

Harold S. Kushner

I have sometimes been wildly, despairingly, acutely
miserable, racked with sorrow, but through it all I still
know quite certainly that just to be alive is a grand thing.

Agatha Christie

If you bless a situation, it has no power to hurt you, and
even if it is troublesome for a time, it will gradually fade
out, if you sincerely bless it.

Emmet Fox

Grace strikes us when we are in great pain and restlessness.
Sometimes at that moment a wave of light breaks into our darkness,
and it is as though a voice were saying: "You are accepted."

Paul Johannes Tillich

I've missed more than 9,000 shots in my career. I've lost almost 300 games. Twenty-six times, I've been trusted to take the game winning shot and missed. I've failed over and over and over again in my life. And that is why I succeed.

Michael Jordan

Ask, and it shall be given to you; seek, and ye shall find; knock, and it shall be opened unto you.

Matthew 7:7

Difficult times have helped me to
understand better than before how
infinitely rich and beautiful life is in
every way and that so many things
that one goes worrying about are of
no importance whatsoever.

Isak Dinesen

❖

There are some things you learn best in
calm, and some in storm.

Anaïs Nin

I don't know the key to success, but the key to failure is to try to please everyone. Bill Cosby

❖

You may encounter many defeats
but you must not be defeated.
In fact, the encountering may be
the very experience which creates
the vitality and the power to endure.
Maya Angelou

When one door of happiness closes, another opens;

but often we look so long at the closed door that we do not see

the one which has been opened for us.

Helen Keller

I think the person who has had more experience of hardships
can stand more firmly in the face of problems than the person
who has never experienced suffering. From this angle then,
some suffering can be a good lesson for life.

His Holiness the Dalai Lama

✹

Being brave can be a very complex
matter.... You have to realize that,
most of the time when you take a risk
and follow your instincts, you have
probably made the right decision.
In the end, you win out.

Aida Alvarez, Former Director of the Small Business Administration

God shall wipe all tears from their eyes;
and there shall be no more death, nor crying,
nether shall there be any more pain:
for the former things are passed away.

Revelations 21:14

A successful man is one who can lay a firm foundation
with the bricks others have thrown at him.

David Brinkley

Man's greatest actions are performed
in minor struggles. Life, misfortune,
isolation, abandonment and poverty are
battlefields which have their heroes—
obscure heroes who are at times greater
than illustrious heroes.

Victor Hugo

Birds sing after a storm;
why shouldn't people feel as free
to delight in whatever remains to them?

Rose F. Kennedy

Everyone is our brother or sister in suffering. No one comes to us from a home which has never known sorrow. They come to help us because they too know what it feels like to be hurt by life.

Harold S. Kushner

❧

I remember when I was in college, people told me I couldn't play in the NBA. There's always somebody saying you can't do it, and those people have to be ignored.

Bill Cartwright, center for the NBA-champion Chicago Bulls

Be bold. If you're going
to make an error, make a
doozey, and don't be
afraid to hit the ball.

Billie Jean King

I have learned silence from the talkative; tolerance from
the intolerant and kindness from the unkind. I should not
be ungrateful to those teachers.

Kahlil Gibran

I believe that unarmed truth and
unconditional love will have the final
word in reality. That is why right,
temporarily defeated, is stronger than
evil triumphant.

Martin Luther King, Jr.

❦

The way I see it, if you want the rainbow,
you gotta put up with the rain.

Dolly Parton

The mountain remains unmoved at seeming defeat by the mist.

Rabindranath Tagore

The greatest glory in living lies
not in never falling, but in rising
every time we fall.

Nelson Mandela

1) Always do your best, that's good enough.

2) Never throw away your tomorrows worrying about yesterday.

3) The day you see the truth and cease to speak is the day you die.

4) If you want to get out of the cotton patch, you have to get something in your head.

Sharecropper,
and mother of Dr. Joycelyn Elders, former U.S. Surgeon General

❋

In the midst of winter, I found there was,
within me, an invincible summer.

Albert Camus

Turn your wounds into wisdom.

Oprah Winfrey

✳

Age is no barrier. It's a limitation you put on your mind.

Jackie Joyner-Kersee

✳

Sometimes our light goes out but is blown into
flame by an encounter with another human being.
Each of us owes the deepest thanks to those
who have kindled this inner light.

Albert Schweitzer

People are like stained-glass windows.
They sparkle and shine when the sun is out,
but when the darkness sets in,
their true beauty is revealed only
if there is a light within.

Elisabeth Kübler-Ross

I've always made a total effort, even when
the odds seemed entirely against me.
I never quit trying; I never felt that
I didn't have a chance to win.

Arnold Palmer

I have learned that success is to be measured not so much
by the position one has reached in life as by the obstacles
he has overcome while trying to succeed.

Booker T. Washington

The reward of suffering is experience.

Aeschylus

If you have no confidence in self, you are twice defeated in the race of life. With confidence, you have won even before you have started.

Marcus Garvey

How strange this fear of death is! We are never frightened at a sunset.

George Macdonald

Ah, but a man's reach should exceed his grasp, Or what's a heaven for?

Robert Browning

Aerodynamically, the bumble bee shouldn't be able to fly, but the bumble bee doesn't know it so it goes on flying anyway. Mary Kay Ash

Success is going from
failure to failure without
a loss of enthusiasm.   Sir Winston Churchill

Life never presents us with anything which may not be looked
upon as a fresh starting point, no less than as a termination.
André Gide

A stumble may prevent a fall.
Thomas Fuller

Yield not thy neck
To fortune's yoke, but let thy dauntless mind
Still ride in triumph over all mischance.

William Shakespeare

One may walk over
the highest mountain
one step at a time.

Barbara Walters

Every sweet hath its sour; every evil its good. Ralph Waldo Emerso

✳

In the difficult are the friendly
forces, the hands that work on us.
Rainer Maria Rilke

✳

Just don't give up trying to do what
you really want to do. Where there is
love and inspiration, I don't think you
can go wrong.

Ella Fitzgerald

There are no shortcuts
to any place worth going.

Beverly Sills

We have but two lives. The life we learn
with and the life we live with after that.

Bernard Malamud, *The Natural*

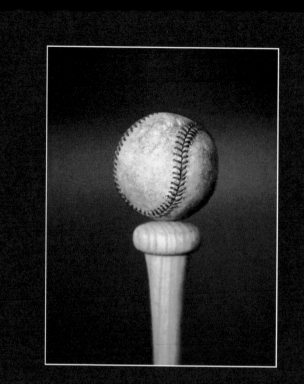

My motto was always to keep swinging.
Whether I was in a slump or feeling badly
or having trouble off the field,
the only thing to do was keep swinging.

Hank Aaron

Flops are a part of life's menu and
I've never been a girl to miss out
on any of the courses.

Rosalind Russell

Life has no smooth road for any of us;
and in the bracing atmosphere
of a high aim the very roughness
stimulates the climber to steadier steps
'til the legend, "over steep ways
to the stars," fulfills itself.

William C. Doane

Champions keep
playing until they
get it right.

Billie Jean King

It is right it should be so,
Man was made for joy and woe;
And when this we rightly know,
Through the world we safely go.

William Blake

No traveler e'er reached that blest abode who found not thorns and briers in his road.

William Cowper

Here is a rule to remember when anything tempts you to feel bitter: not, "This is a misfortune," but "To bear this worthily is good fortune."

Marcus Aurelius

Setting a goal is not the main thing. It is deciding how you will go about achieving it and staying with that plan. Tom Landry

Do not weep; do not wax indignant.
Understand.

Baruch Spinoza

There is nothing so bitter that a patient mind cannot find
some solace for it.

Marcus Annaeus Seneca

Our real blessings often appear
to us in the shape of pains, losses
and disappointments.

Joseph Addison

Many a man curses the rain that falls
upon his head, and knows not that it
brings abundance to drive away hunger.

Saint Basil

My friends have made the story of my life. In a thousand ways they have turned my limitations into beautiful privileges, and enabled me to walk serene and happy in the shadow cast by my deprivation.

Helen Keller

There is in the worst of fortune the best of chances for a happy change.

Euripides

Be not overcome of evil,

but overcome evil with good.

Romans

There is no fruit which is not bitter
before it is ripe.

Publilius Syrus

You must lose a fly
to catch a trout.

George Herbert

The man who is swimming against the stream knows the strength of it.

Woodrow Wilson

✯

The humblest citizen of
all the land, when clad in
the armor of a righteous
cause, is stronger than all
the hosts of error.

William Jennings Bryant

✯

Grief should be the instructor of the wise;
Sorrow is Knowledge.

Lord Byron

Every exit is an entry somewhere else.

Tom Stoppard

It is better to drink of deep griefs than to taste shallow pleasures.

William Hazlitt

Hearts live
by being wounded.

Oscar Wilde

We are not here to curse the darkness, but to light the candle that can guide us through that darkness to a safe and sane future.

John F. Kennedy

Weeping may endure for a night,
but joy cometh in the morning.

Psalms

Sadness flies away on the wings of time.

Jean de la Fontaine

Everything in life that we really accept
undergoes a change. So suffering must
become love. That is the mystery.

Katherine Mansfield

One day in retrospect
the years of struggle will
strike you as the most
beautiful.

Sigmund
Freud

❋

Don't cry because it's over. Smile because it happened.

Dr. Seuss

✳

Although the world is full of suffering,
it is also full of the overcoming of it.

Helen Keller

✳

They that sow in tears, shall reap in joy.

Psalm 126

Knowing sorrow well,
I learn the way to succor the distressed.   Virgil

Through loyalty to the past, our mind refuses to realize that tomorrow's joy
is possible only if today's makes way for it; that each wave owes the beauty
of its line only to the withdrawal of the preceding one.

André Gide

Many a green isle needs must be
In the deep wide sea of Misery,
Or the mariner, worn and wan,
Never thus could voyage on.

Percy Bysshe Shelley

Hold your head high, stick your chest out.
You can make it. It gets dark sometimes
but morning comes…. Keep hope alive.

Jesse Jackson

If there is a sin against life, it consists perhaps not so much
in despairing of life as in hoping for another life and in
eluding the implacable grandeur of this life.

Albert Camus

I accept the Universe. Margaret Fuller

Sorrows remembered sweeten present joy.

Robert Pollok

We do not succeed in changing things according to our desire, but gradually our desire changes. The situation that we hoped to change because it was intolerable becomes unimportant. We have not managed to surmount the obstacle, as we were absolutely determined to do, but life has taken us round it, led us past it, and then if we turn round to gaze at the remote past, we can barely catch sight of it, so imperceptible has it become.

Marcel Proust

✫

We cannot learn without pain.
Aristotle

Life, believe, is not a dream
So dark as sages say;
Oft a little morning sun
Foretells a pleasant day.

Charlotte Brontë

✯

Never yet was a springtime,
Late though lingered the snow,
That the sap stirred not at the whisper
Of the southwind, sweet and low;
Never yet was a springtime when
the buds forgot to blow.

Margaret E. Sangster

I know why the caged bird sings, ah me,

When his wing is bruised and his bosom sore, —

When he beats his bars and would be free;

It is not a carol of joy or glee,

But a prayer that he sends from his heart's deep core,

But a plea, that upward to Heaven, he flings —

I know why the caged bird sings!

Paul Laurence Dunbar

❖

Out of the night that covers me,

Black as the pit from pole to pole,

I thank whatever gods may be

For my unconquerable soul.

William Ernest Henley

All mankinde is of one Author,
and is one volume; when one
Man dies, one Chapter is not
torne out of the book, but
translated into a better language.

John Donne

When the dust settles and the pages of
history are written, it will not be the
angry defenders of intolerance who have
made the difference. That reward will go
to those who dared to step outside the
safety of their privacy in order to expose
and rout the prevailing prejudices.

John Shelby Spong

If love is at the core of us, we can add love
to any misery we feel. Hugh Prather,
Notes to Myself

In time, I hope and believe the anguish with you will be
covered over. That is the only way to express it. It is like
new skin covering a wound. That doesn't mean that one
forgets the people who have gone away.

Edith Sitwell

Difficulty, my brethren, is the nurse of greatness.
A harsh nurse, who roughly rocks her foster children
into strength and athletic proportion.

William Cullen Bryant

The Lord is my shepherd; I shall not want.
He maketh me to lie down in green pastures: he leadeth me beside the still waters.
He restoreth my soul: he leadeth me in the paths of righteousness for his name's sake.
Yea, though I walk through the valley of the shadow of death,
I will fear no evil: for thou art with me: thy rod and thy staff they comfort me...
Surely goodness and mercy shall follow me all the days of life:
and I will dwell in the house of the Lord for ever.

Psalm 23

Grief melts away
Like snow in May,
As if there were no such cold thing.

George Herbert

It is always darkest just before the day dawneth.

Thomas Fuller

★

If we had no winter, the spring
would not be so pleasant:
if we did not sometimes taste of adversity,
prosperity would not be so welcome.

Anne Bradstreet

★

A man should never be ashamed to own when he has been
in the wrong, which is but saying, in other words, that he
is wiser today than he was yesterday.

Alexander Pope

A talent is formed in stillness,
a character in the world's torrent.

Johann Wolfgang von Goethe

There is in every woman's heart a spark
of heavenly fire, which lies dormant in
the broad daylight of prosperity; but
which kindles up, and beams and blazes
in the dark hour of adversity.

Washington Irving

Happiness is beneficial for the body but it is grief that develops the powers of the mind.

Marcel Proust

God does not ask the impossible.

Canon law

Some steps must be taken defiantly,
against the grain. There is no growth
without a bursting, without pain.

John Updike

✳

I bend but do not break.

Jean de la Fontaine

Lead, kindly Light, amid the encircling gloom;

Lead thou me on!

The night is dark, and I am far from home;

Lead thou me on!

Keep thou my feet: I do not ask to see

The distant scene; one step enough for me.

Cardinal Newman

PERSISTENCE

Have patience with everything unresolved
in your heart and try to love the questions
themselves as if they were locked rooms or books
written in a very foreign language. Don't search for
the answers, which could not be given you now,
because you would not be able to live them.
And the point is, to live everything.
Live the questions now. Perhaps then, someday far
in the future, you will gradually, without even
noticing it, live your way into the answer.

Rainer Maria Rilke

Keep away from those who try to belittle your ambitions.
Small people always do that, but the really great make you
believe that you too can become great.

Mark Twain

It is never too late to be what you might have been.

George Eliot

Let no one be discouraged by the belief there is nothing one person can do against the enormous array of the world's ills, misery, ignorance, and violence. Few will have the greatness to bend history, but each of us can work to change a small portion of events. And in the total of all those acts will be written the history of a generation.

Robert Kennedy

The future belongs to those who believe in the beauty of the dream.

Eleanor Roosevelt

Inside of a ring or out,
ain't nothing wrong with going down.
It's staying down that's wrong.

Muhammad Ali

By seeing the seed of failure in every success,
we remain humble. By seeing the seed of success
in every failure we remain hopeful.

Mel Ziegler, founder of Banana Republic

Consult not your fears but your hopes and your dreams.
Think not about your frustrations, but about your unful-
filled potential. Concern yourself not with what you tried
and failed in, but with what it is still possible for you to do.

Pope John XIII

🌹

Tomorrow is a new day
You shall begin it serenely
And with too high a spirit
To be encumbered by
Your old nonsense.

Ralph Waldo Emerson

Whatever you can do or dream you can, begin it;

Boldness has genius, power and magic in it.

Johann Wolfgang von Goethe

We can't take any credit

for our talents. It's how

we use them that counts.

Madeleine L'Engle

Life is either a daring adventure or nothing. To keep our

faces toward change and behave like free spirits in the

presence of fate is strength undefeatable.

Helen Keller

You gain strength, courage, and confidence by every experience in which you really stop to look fear in the face. You must do the thing you cannot do.

Eleanor Roosevelt

All serious daring starts from within.

Eudora Welty

Nothing in the world can take the place of Persistence.

Talent will not; nothing is more commonplace than unsuccessful men with talent.

Genius will not; unrewarded genius is almost a proverb.

Education alone will not; the world is full of educated derelicts.

Persistence and Determination alone are omnipotent.

Calvin Coolidge

You're braver than you believe, and
stronger than you seem, and smarter
than you think.

A.A. Milne

★

Your mental state should always remain calm.

Even if some anxiety occurs, as it is bound to in life, you should always remain calm.

Like a wave, which rises from the water and dissolves back into the water,

these disturbances are very short,

so they should not affect your basic mental attitude.

His Holiness the Dalai Lama

✹

You can do some crazy things when you believe.

Every human being on this earth has a purpose.

Everyone has something they can give.

The need is there and you rise to the need.

Sheila Coates,

activist, founder of Black Women United for Action

Twenty years from now you will be
more disappointed by the things
you didn't do than by the ones you did.
So throw off the bowlines,
Sail away from the safe harbor.
Catch the trade winds in your sails.
Explore. Dream.

Mark Twain

When you get into a tight place, and everything
goes against you, till it seems as though you could
not hold on a moment longer, never give up then —
for that is just the place and time that the tide will turn.

Harriet Beecher Stowe

Success isn't something you chase.
It's something you have to put forth
the effort for constantly. Then maybe
it'll come when you least expect it.
Most people don't understand that.

Michael Jordan

Shoot for the moon. Even if you miss,
you will land among the stars.

Les Brown

✭

Many of life's failures are people who did not realize how
close they were to success when they gave up.

Thomas A. Edison

Let your hook be always cast;
in the pool where you least
expect it, there will be a fish.

Ovid

Never give in —
never, never, never, never.

Winston Churchill

A dream doesn't become reality through magic; it takes sweat, determination and hard work.

Colin Powell

Never let your head hang down.
Never give up and sit down and grieve.
Find another way.

Leroy "Satchel" Paige

I was taught that the way of progress is neither swift nor easy.

Marie Curie

Pay no attention to what the critics say; no statue has ever been erected to a critic.

Jean Sibelius

Life is about not knowing, having to change, taking the moment and making the best of it, without knowing what's going to happen next.

Gilda Radner

I dance to the tune that is played

Spanish proverb

❁

Life only demands from you the strength you possess.
Only one feat is possible—not to have run away.

Dag Hammarskjöld

❁

A life spent in making mistakes is not
only more honorable but more useful than
a life spent doing nothing.

George Bernard Shaw

Experience is not what happens to you;
it is what you do with what happens to you.

Aldous Huxley

There is no failure except
in no longer trying

Elbert Hubbard

The best thing we can
do is to make wherever
we're lost look as much
like home as we can.

Christopher Fry

God is our refuge and strength,
a very present help in trouble.

Psalms

One doesn't discover new lands without consenting to lose
sight of the shore for a very long time.

André Gide

Self-respect will keep a man from being abject
when he is in the power of enemies,
and will enable him to feel that he may be
in the right when the world is against him.

Bertrand Russell

There is no success without hardship.

Sophocles

The brilliant passes, like the dew at morn;

The true endures, for ages yet unborn.

Johann Wolfgang von Goethe

❖

Grieve not, because thou understandest not life's mystery;

behind the veil is concealed many a delight.

Hafiz

❖

Vision is the art of seeing things invisible.

Jonathan Swift

Vitality shows in not only the ability to persist but the ability to start over.

F. Scott Fitzgerald

Nothing is impossible to a willing heart.

John Heywood

Let a man in a garret but burn
with enough intensity and he will
set fire to the world.

Antoine de Saint-Exupéry

Nothing splendid has ever been achieved except by those who dared believe that something inside them was superior to circumstances.

Bruce Barton

Somewhere, in the back of your
mind, try to remember that
everything has God's fingerprints
on it. The fact that we can't see
the beauty in something doesn't
suggest that it's not there.
Rather, it suggests that we are
not looking carefully enough
or with a broad enough
perspective to see it.

Richard Carlson,

Don't Sweat the Small Stuff

 He that can have patience can have what he will.

Benjamin Franklin

The race is not to the swift, nor the battle to the strong.

Ecclesiastes 9:11

✹

Great things are not done by
impulse, but by a series of small
things brought together.

Vincent van Gogh

Every experience in life, everything with
which we have come in contact in life, is a
chisel which has been cutting away at our
life statue, molding, modifying, shaping it.
We are part of all we have met.
Everything we have seen, heard, felt, or
thought has had its hand in molding us,
shaping us.

Orison Swett Marden

✳

I think and think for months, for years.
Ninety-nine times the conclusion is false.
The hundredth time I am right.

Albert Einstein

It is a mistake to
look too far ahead.
Only one link in the
chain of destiny can be
handled at a time.

Winston Churchill

છ

Take your needle, my child, and work at
your pattern; it will come out a rose by
and by. Life is like that; one stitch at a
time taken patiently, and the pattern will
come out all right, like embroidery.

Oliver Wendell
Holmes

Nothing can be done except little by little.

Charles Baudelaire

ॐ

Great works are performed not only by
strength, but by perserverance.

Samuel Johnson

ॐ

The secret of success is constancy of purpose.

Benjamin Disraeli

Let me tell you the secret that has led me to my goal:
my strength lies solely in my tenacity.

Louis Pasteur

❋

There are no shorcuts to any place worth going. Beverly Sills

❋

He turns not back who is bound to a star.

Leonardo da Vinci

Life is a festival only to the wise.

Ralph Waldo Emerson

Two things fill my mind with ever-increasing
wonder and awe: The starry heavens above me
and the moral law within me.

ॐ   Immanuel Kant

To live is to change, and to be perfect is
to have changed often.

John Henry Newman

Great passions may give us this quickened
sense of life, ecstasy and sorrow of love,
the various forms of enthusiastic activity,
disinterested or otherwise, which come
naturally to many of us.

Walter Pater

It takes a very long time
to become young.

Pablo Picasso

Without passion man is a mere latent
force and possibility, like the flint which
awaits the shock of the iron before it can
give forth its spark.

Henri Frederic Amiel

⭐

Understanding is the
reward of faith.
Therefore seek not to
understand that thou
mayest believe, but
believe that thou
mayest understand.

Saint Augustine

No coward soul is mine,

No trembler in the world's storm-troubled sphere:

I see Heaven's glories shine,

And faith shines equal, arming me from fear.

Emily Brontë

Man is only truly great when he acts from the passions.

Benjamin Disraeli

❧

Dare to be wrong
and to dream.

Friedrich von Schiller

Hitch your wagon to a star.

Ralph Waldo Emerson

No seed shall perish which
the soul hath sown.

John Addington Symonds

Be not afraid of life. Believe that life is worth living,
and your belief will help create the fact.

William James

We are all in the gutter, but some of us
are looking at the stars.

Oscar Wilde

❖

Fate often saves an undoomed warrior
when his courage endures.

Beowulf

Speak boldly, and speak truly,
Shame the devil.

John Fletcher

❖

Victory is a thing of the will.
Ferdinand Foch

❖

Fear is a greater evil than the evil itself.
St. François de Sales

One person with a belief is a social power
equal to ninety-nine who have only interests.

John Stuart Mill

✳

Forget thy tongue on an anvil of truth
And what flies up, though it be but a
spark, shall have weight.

Pindar

Dare to do things worthy of imprisonment
if you mean to be of consequence.

Juvenal

✳

Where the willingness is great,
the difficulties cannot be great.

Machiavelli

The finest edge is made with
the blunt whetstone.

Richard Hooker

🌀

It is by presence of mind in untried emergencies
that the native metal of a man is tested.

Abraham
Lincoln

🌀

Greatness is a road leading towards the unknown.

Charles de Gaulle

❆

If there is no struggle, there is no progress.   Frederick Douglass

❆

Better incur the trouble of testing and
exploding a thousand fallacies than by
rejecting stifle a single beneficent Truth.
Horace Greeley

We will either find a way or make one.

Hannibal

The troubles of our proud and angry dust
Are from eternity, and shall not fail.
Bear them we can, and if we can we must.
Shoulder the sky, my lad, and drink your ale.

A.E. Housman

Nothing is impossible to industry.

Periander

❖

I can, therefore I am.

Simone Weil

Let nothing disturb you
Let nothing affright you
All things are passing;
God never changes.
Patient endurance attains all things.

St. Teresa of Avila

❧

To every thing there is a season, and a
time to every purpose under the heaven.

Ecclesiastes 3:1

Wisdom begins with sacrifice of immediate pleasures for long-range purposes.

Louis Finkelstein

The more the marble wastes,

the more the statue grows.

Michelangelo

Possess your soul with patience. John Dryden

You have to study a great

deal to know a little.

Montesquieu

We sometimes had those little rubs
which Providence sends to enhance
the value of its favors.

Oliver Goldsmith

Large streams from little fountains flow,

Tall oaks from little acorns grow.

David Everett

Come one, come all!

this rock shall fly

From its firm base as soon as I.

Sir Walter Scott

✭

Be always sure you're right—then go ahead.

Davy Crockett

Damn the torpedos—full speed ahead! David Glasgow Farragut

★

If the single man plant himself
indomitably on his instincts,
and there abide, the huge world
will come round to him.

Ralph Waldo Emerson

Though I sit down now,
the time will come when you will hear me.

Benjamin Disraeli

To endure is greater than to dare;
to tire out hostile fortune; to be daunted
by no difficulty; to keep heart when
all have lost it; to go through intrigue
spotless; to forego even ambition
when the end is gained—
who can say this is not greatness?

William Thackeray

The swiftest traveler is he that goes afoot.

Henry David
Thoreau

I am only one,

But still I am one.

I cannot do everything,

But still I can do something;

And because I cannot do everything

I will not refuse to do the something that I can do.

Edward Everett Hale

Genius is one per cent inspiration and
ninety-nine percent perspiration.

Thomas A. Edison

The ripest peach is highest in the tree.

James Whitcomb Riley